Contents

MW01131785

Introduction

Have you ever seen those guitarists that sound like they know exactly what they're doing when they're improvising? They just seem to hit all the right notes while their playing sounds crisp and melodic, as if they'd planned it all out beforehand, or were born with a God-given sense of melody. I'd always wondered how on earth they were able to come up with such melodic and flowing lines, thinking that they must simply be gifted, or have done some serious woodshedding. Then, during one unforgettable class at music college the door was opened to a method for playing and thinking as melodically and as effortlessly as they did, and this is what I want to share with you in this eBook.

As this eBook provides another perspective on improvising, it can be used by guitarists of any level from beginners who have begun to explore scales, right up to intermediate and advanced players who are perhaps looking to become more melodic, go beyond scale patterns, or have far more control over what they play when improvising.

This eBook is based on a 10-day program studying and practicing the material for approximately 2 hours a day. As everyone works at a different pace, you may be able to accomplish more in one day than is scheduled in the eBook; this is fine as long as you have really internalized the information before moving on. If you've been playing for just a year or two, then you may find you need to spend a couple of days for each 'Day' in the eBook; this is fine too as the point is to understand and internalize the material, not rush to the end. It's also important not to skip days as all the exercises must be completed in the order given for the material to be truly effective.

There are four backing tracks based on the four triads which are the foundation for all the scales in the book, and these can be downloaded from the site (see link below).

Good luck, and here's to some great melodic soloing!

Matt

http://www.unlocktheguitar.net/backing-tracks.html

Day 1

The Minor Triad contains the intervals 1, b3 (flat 3) and 5 (perfect fifth). The intervals of a minor triad, or any triad for that matter, are always the same regardless of the starting note.

Step 1 is to familiarize yourself with the location of each 1, b3, and 5 on the fretboard in any given key. We'll use G for the purposes of this eBook, but remember that you can easily move this information to other tonalities as what changes are the notes, not the intervals.

In the following fretboard diagram, you'll see the intervals 1, b3, 5 in G. Use the backing track to familiarize yourself with the sound and their location, but try not to rely on any shapes you may already know. Move from one note to the next horizontally, vertically and diagonally, naming each interval as you go. Take your time by doing this in an almost meditative way.

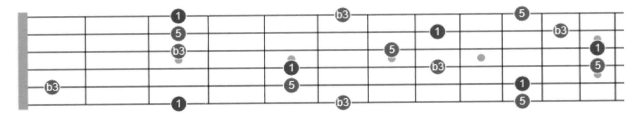

In **Step 2** we add in the b7 interval. Repeat the above process for each new interval you add in, and above all, don't rush it.

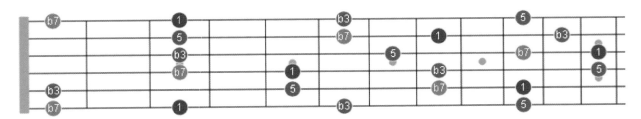

When you're ready for the next interval, add in the 4 as follows.

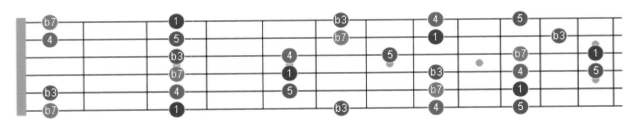

You may have realized that you're now playing the good old G Minor Pentatonic Scale, but from a completely different perspective! Your playing should be much more melodic, and you should feel much more in control of what you're playing, and perhaps be catching glimpses of being able to play what you hear in your head. You can probably now also appreciate the difference between mindlessly running up and down a scale pattern, and actually choosing the intervals/notes you want to play to create a specific sound. This is a very powerful technique, indeed!

Interval Awareness: b7 (the flat seven)

To strengthen our knowledge of interval location for those intervals not included in the triads, we need to get used to their location in relation to the root. What we want to be able to do is to know where these intervals are either below or above the root interval.

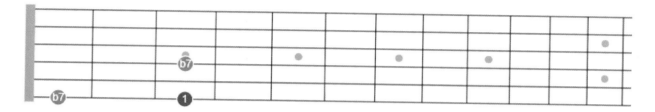

These interval locations are also the same when the root is on the A string:

However, when we move this across to the D and B strings we invoke the 'warp factor' which means that the interval on the B string moves up a semi-tone, or one fret, due to the guitar's tuning:

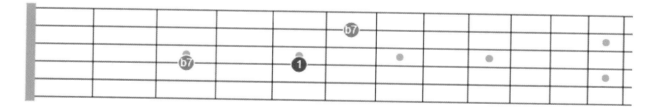

Moving over to the G and E strings, the interval locations remain consistent, and as we're now in the middle of the fretboard, another b7 below the root comes into play:

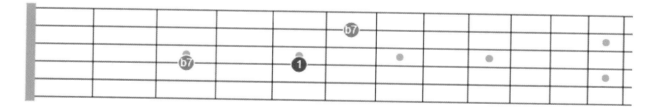

When the root is on the B string, there are b7 intervals on either side:

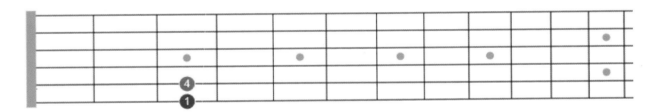

On the E string you get a similar pattern only again it becomes 'warped' by the B string due to the guitar's tuning:

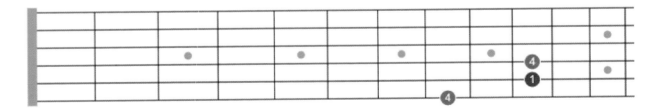

Interval Awareness: 4 (the perfect fourth)

The fourth can be found adjacent to the root on all string pairs, except the G and B strings due once more to the warp factor.

Here it is on the A and D strings with the 4 on the low E string also within easy reach:

On the D and G strings we get the same arrangement:

On the G and B strings we come to the 'bump in the fretboard':

This bump also affects the placement of the 4 below the root on the B string:

And finally, the root on the top E string features two 4 intervals within easy reach:

Day 1 Checkpoint

At this point you should be able move around the pentatonic scale naming each interval as you go; don't worry about speed at this point as speed without accuracy is next to useless.

Day 2

Take a moment to review the minor triad and the process of adding in the 4 and b7 from yesterday using the backing track provided. Be sure to choose the notes you play rather than reverting back to scale patterns.

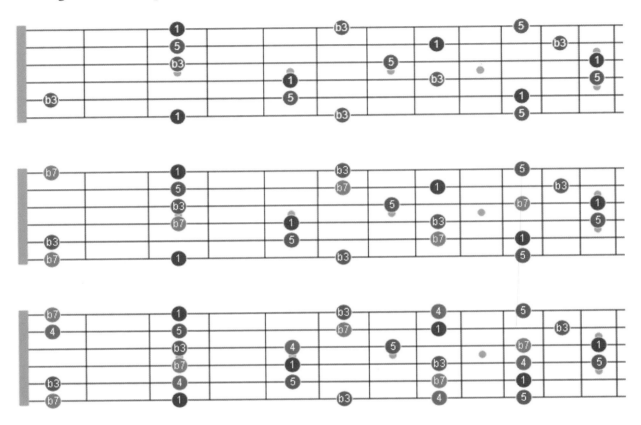

Today we're going to add in two intervals to make the Natural Minor (Aeolian) Scale. First up is the b6 (flat sixth):

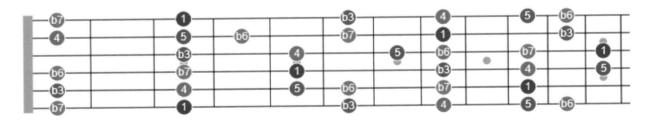

Again, use the backing track provided, meditatively add in the b6. When you're ready, we'll add in the 2:

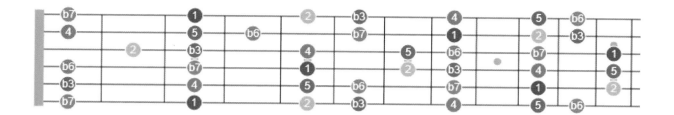

What you now have is the G Natural Minor/Aeolian Scale at your fingertips. Remember to keep choosing the intervals you play instead of reverting back to scale patterns.

Interval Awareness 2 (the two), b6 (the flat six)

Just as we did yesterday, take the time to become aware of where these new intervals are in the relation to the root notes on each string; take each string one at a time and call out the new intervals as you play them. Pay particular attention to how the warp zone area of the B string moves everything up one fret.

Here are all the b6 intervals in relation to the root:

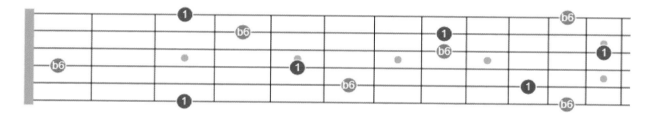

And here are all the 2 intervals in relation to the root:

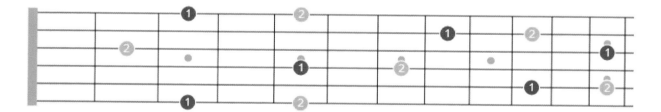

Bear in mind that the 2 is also known as the 9 when it appears in the next octave above. For example, if you were to play the root on the D string and the 2 on the top E string, the 2 would be considered a 9 as it is part of the next octave.

Day 2 Checkpoint

By the end of Day 2 you should be fairly comfortable with the minor pentatonic and the natural minor scale, as well as being able to locate the new intervals: 2 and b6. When you feel ready, move on to Day 3.

Day 3

The Major Triad contains the intervals 1, 3 and 5, and forms the basis for many useful scales and modes. As on Day 1, **Step 1** is to familiarize yourself with the location of each 1, 3, and 5 on the fretboard. In reality you're only really learning one new interval here as you can already locate the 5 with ease.

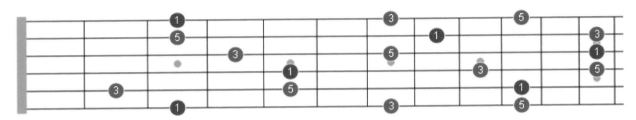

Use the backing track to hear and locate each note of the triad by calling out the interval as you play the note and avoiding any familiar patterns or shapes.

The first interval to add to the major triad is the 6 (natural six) as follows:

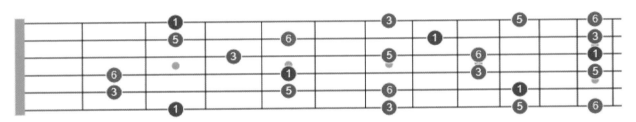

Meditatively combine the natural 6 with the major triad until you can locate each interval with ease. When you're ready, well add in the 2:

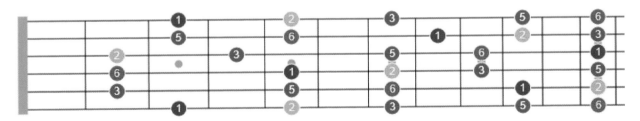

You should now see the G Major Pentatonic Scale appear before your eyes, only now you're in control of the intervals you play, rather than mindlessly firing off bunches of notes! You should also be seeing a very marked difference between running scales and purposely choosing the notes you play. The lack of speed may frustrate you but this will come over time.

Interval Awareness: 6 (the natural six)

Take some time to become familiar with the new interval we added, the natural six, above and below the roots:

Day 3 Checkpoint

By the end of Day 3 you should have learned the major triad and its intervals, plus the location of the natural 6, and another perspective on the Major Pentatonic Scale. When you feel ready, move on to Day 4.

Day 4

On Day 4 we first of all review the Major Triad and the intervals 2 and 6 that we added to it to form the Major Pentatonic Scale:

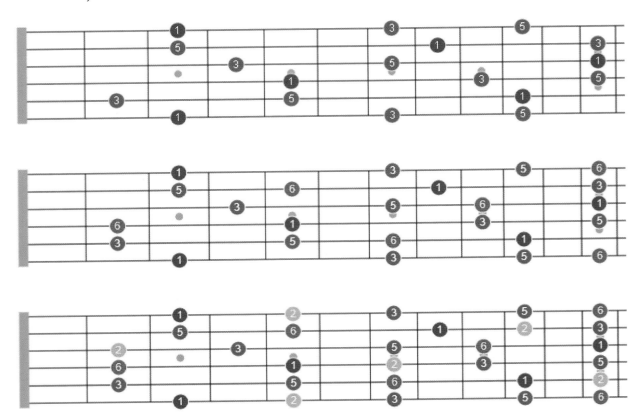

Next we'll add in the 7 (natural seven) which you'll always find on the fret below the root:

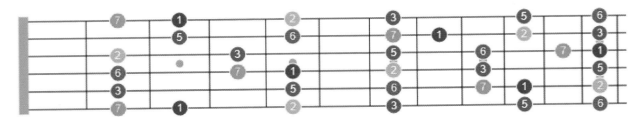

When you're comfortable with the 7, add in the 4 to complete the Major Scale/Ionian Mode:

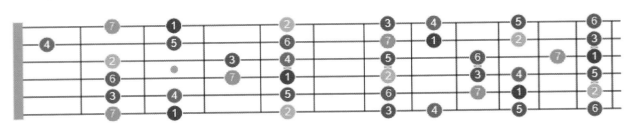

This is a great way to see the major scale as you're no longer a slave to those awkward CAGED patterns or the 3NPS system; we've taken things to the next level by bypassing patterns and choosing the intervals we want to play.

Interval Awareness: 7 (natural seven)

Take a moment to make sure you're aware of where all the 7s are in relation to the root across the fretboard.

Day 4 Checkpoint

We've come such a long way in just four days, and at the end of this fourth day you should be able to play the Major Scale quite comfortably by choosing your intervals, as well as incorporating the location of the natural 7.

Day 5

Along with the Pentatonic Major and Minor Scales, the modes of the Major Scale are the most prominent and useful scales in music. The Major Scale has three major modes and three minor ones, one of which is the major scale itself (the Ionian mode). Today we'll look at how to form the other two major modes: The Lydian and the Mixolydian.

The Lydian Mode

The **Lydian** mode contains the intervals 1, 2, 3, #4, 5, 6, 7 and can be used over major, major 7 and especially major 7b5 chords, so let's start with the major triad:

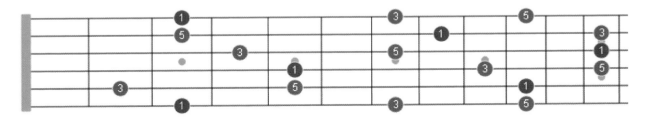

Next, we'll add in a new interval, the #4 as follows:

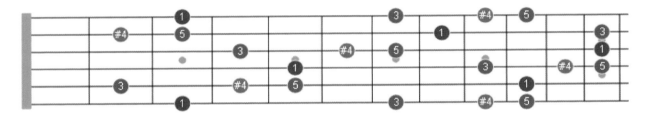

The #4 really defines the Lydian mode so make sure you take your time to hear it in contrast with the major triad.

Next we'll add in the natural 7 as follows:

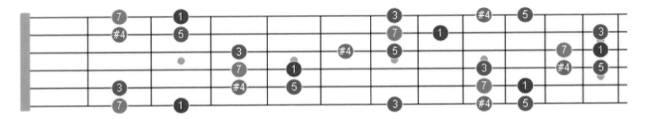

You now have the very essence of the Lydian mode and should be coming up with some interesting, and above all, Lydian sounding stuff, which certainly beats running up and down scale patterns.

Next we add in the 6:

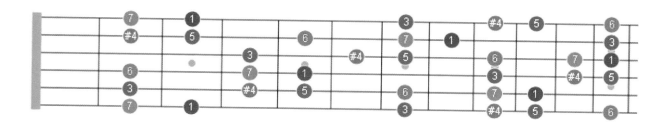

Remember to take your time as you add each note in, there's no rush.

And finally the 2:

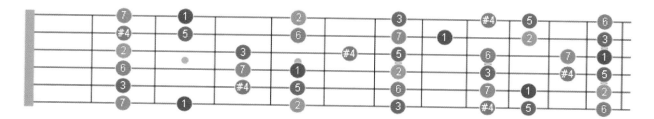

You now have all seven notes that comprise the Lydian scale but with a whole new perspective on how to play them!

The Mixolydian Mode

The other major mode is the Mixolydian Mode and contains the intervals **1, 2, 3, 4, 5, 6, b7**. It has a bright sound and is heavily used in rock and blues over dominant chords.

Let's start with the major triad again:

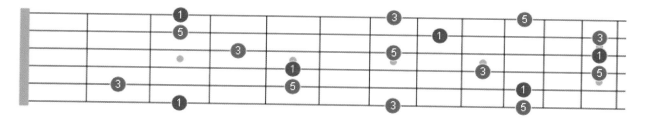

Next we add in the b7. We add the b7 first because like the #4 in the Lydian mode, the b7 really defines the sound of the mode along with the major triad.

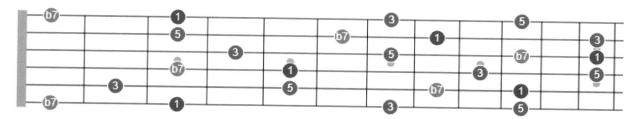

Next we add in the 6:

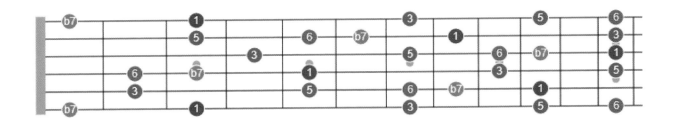

The next interval to add is the 2:

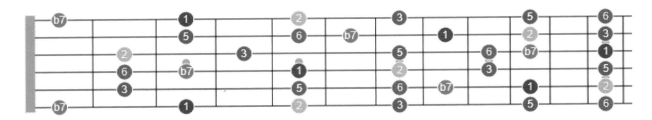

And finally the 4:

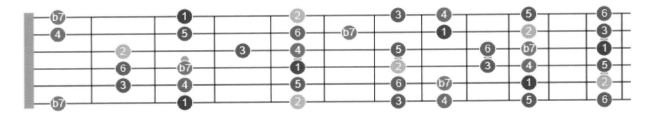

Interval Awareness: #4 (the sharp four)

The Lydian Mode introduced to a new interval, the #4, which you should study in isolation using the following diagram:

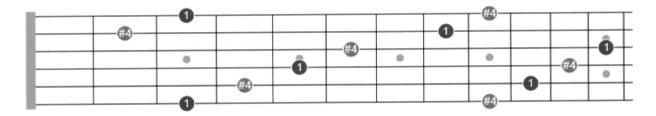

Bonus: The Blues Scale

Since we're looking at the #4, this is a good time to incorporate the Blues Scale which has the intervals: 1, b3, 4, b5, 5, b7. A #4 and a b5 are the same interval, and you would build the blues scale as follows:

First bring out the Minor Triad:

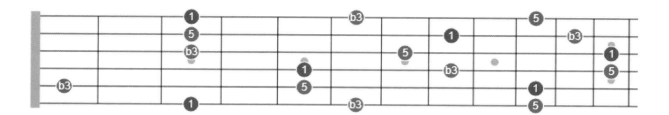

Next we add the b7:

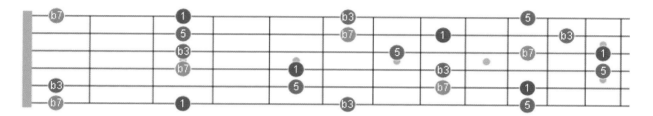

Then the 4 to get the Minor Pentatonic Scale:

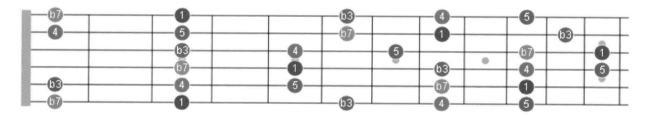

And finally the 'blue' note, the b5:

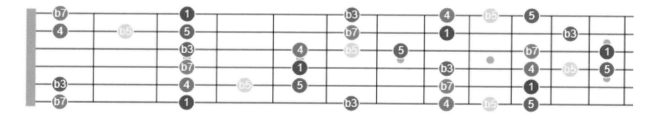

Day 5 Checkpoint

You should now be fairly comfortable with both the Lydian and Mixolydian modes, know what their defining notes are, and be able come up with lines and phrases that draw out their respective sounds.

Day 6

Today we'll look at how to construct the minor modes of the major scale. On Day 2 we looked at the Natural Minor Scale, or the Aeolian mode, which leaves us with two other minor modes: The Dorian Mode and the Phrygian Mode.

The Dorian Mode

This minor mode is made up of the following intervals: **1, 2, b3, 4, 5, 6, b7**. The characteristic note of this scale is the natural 6, so our construction process will be as follows:

We start with the Minor Triad:

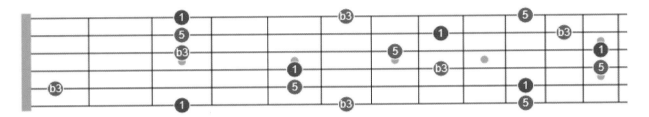

Then we add the 6 as this interval really defines the sound of the Dorian Mode:

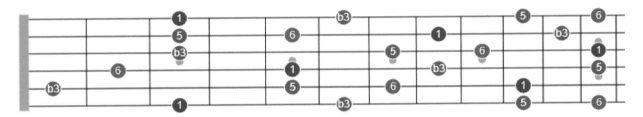

Then the b7:

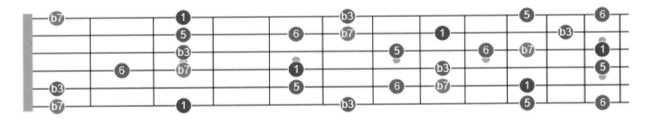

Then the 2:

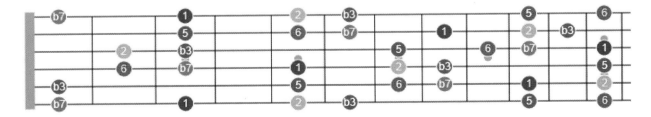

And finally the 4:

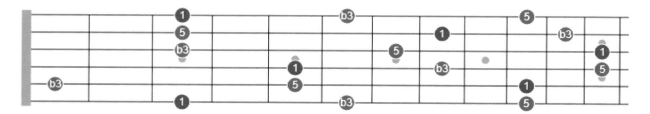

The Phrygian Mode

This minor mode includes our final interval, the b2, which is easy to remember as it's always right next to the root.

To build the Phrygian scale, begin with the Minor Triad:

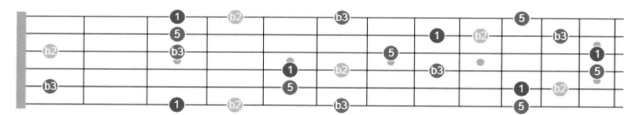

Next we add in the b2, the note that defines the Phrygian Mode:

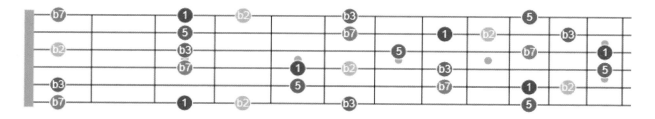

Then the b7:

Next up is the b6:

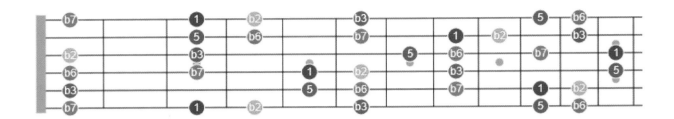

And finally the 4:

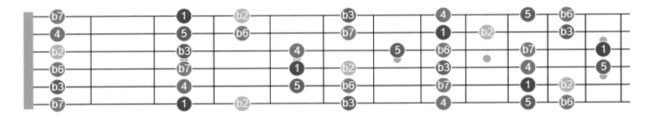

Interval Awareness: b2 (the flat two)

Our last new interval is the b2, so spend a little time making yourself aware of its locations on the fretboard. Use the following diagram:

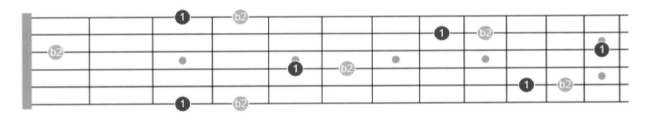

Day 6 Checkpoint

You should now be familiar with the Dorian and Phrygian Modes, and be able to construct them at will using their corresponding interval formulas.

Day 7

The last mode of the Major Scale is the Locrian mode. Unlike the major and minor modes, the Locrian Mode is based off a Diminished Triad, which contains the intervals **1, b3, b5**. The Locrian Mode itself contains the intervals **1, b2, b3, 4, b5, b6, b7.**

Here it is on the fretboard for you to learn the interval locations. This shouldn't take you too long as we've already studied these intervals extensively.

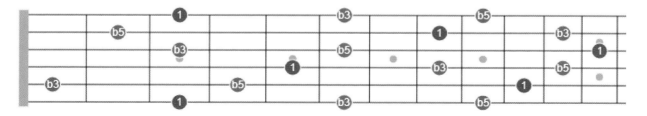

The Locrian Mode

To form the Locrian Mode, we add the following intervals to the diminished triad above:

First we'll add in the b2:

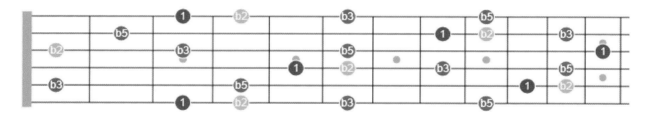

Next we add in the b7:

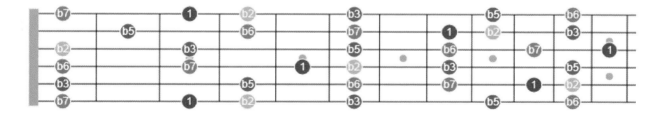

Next we add in the b6:

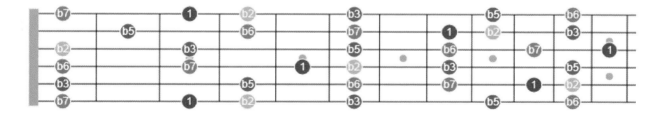

And finally we add in the 4:

This gives us the Locrian Mode, which can be used for playing over diminished and m7b5 chords. You may have noticed that if there's an unaltered 4, we normally add it last; this is because an unaltered 4 is the interval that has the least effect over the general sound of a scale or mode.

Day 7 Checkpoint

By the end of Day 7 you should be familiar with both the Diminished Triad and the Locrian Mode.

Day 8

Our last triad type is the Augmented Triad, which doesn't really appear in a lot of scales but is useful nonetheless. It contains the intervals 1, 3, #5, and this is what it looks like on the fretboard:

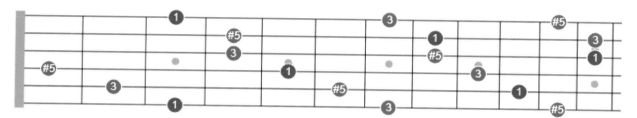

You may not recognize the #5, but it's not a new interval; it is in fact the same as a b6 but for the sake of triad spelling (these must be spelled with the numbers 1, 3, 5) it is known as a #5.

The Lydian Augmented Scale

The third mode of the Melodic Minor Scale, the Lydian Augmented Scale, is based off an Augmented Triad. To build it on the fretboard first start with the Augmented Triad above and then add the following intervals; #4, 7, 6, 2.

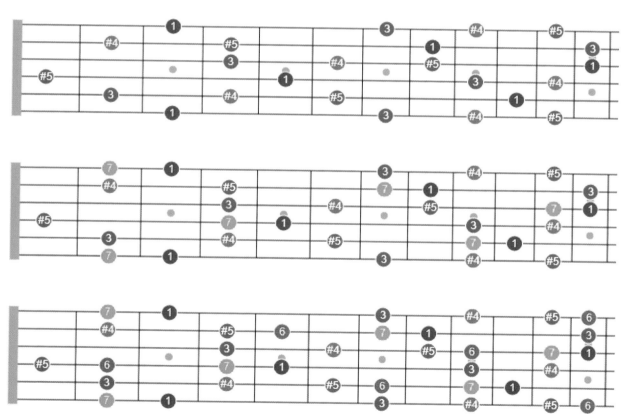

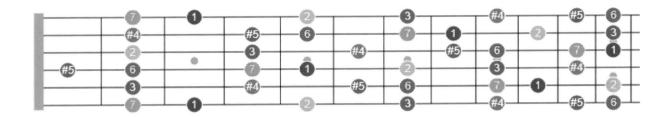

The Ionian #5 Scale

Another mode that's based off an Augmented Triad is the Ionian #5, the third mode of the Harmonic Minor. As the name suggests, it's a Major Scale with a #5 instead of a 5. To build it on the fretboard first start with the Augmented Triad above and then add the following intervals: 7, 6, 2, 4.

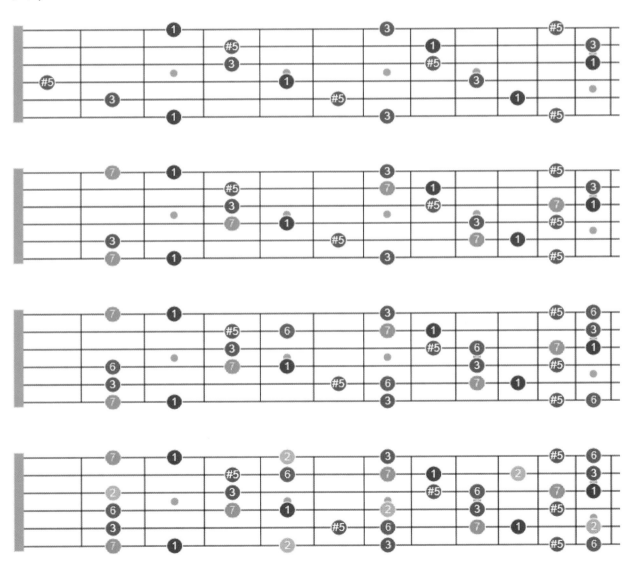

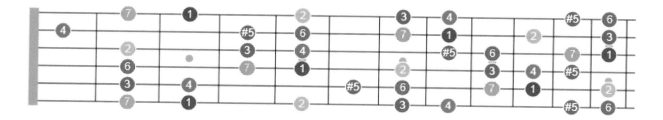

Day 8 Checkpoint

At this point you should be very comfortable with finding intervals and the four triad types. You should also be able to move around the fretboard quite freely using intervals.

Day 9

By now you should have a pretty good idea of how to move around the fretboard using intervals, and you should be getting quicker at it. Day 9 is a good time to practice moving this information to other tonalities, especially the four types of triad. Remember that all interval locations in relation to the root are exactly the same in any tonality, it's only the notes underneath them that change.

Another task for today is to practice using the backing tracks, but without following any specific scale, that is, if you're playing over the minor backing track, you choose the intervals you want to play and see what you can come up with. This exercise is essential to make sure your ear is involved in what you're playing, and to close the gap between what you hear in your head and what your fingers are playing.

Day 10

Congratulations on reaching this point in the eBook, all your hard work over the last week or so has led to a new way of seeing the fretboard and how you can dictate what you want to play, rather than being a slave to endless scale patterns!

From now on, if you want to learn an arpeggio or scale, or even come up with your own chord shapes, simply look up the intervals and break them down into steps as we did with the Pentatonic Scales and each of the Modes.

The following table summarizes the steps we went through for each mode: Start with the triad, either major, minor, augmented or diminished, then in Step 2 add the note that defines the scale or mode, so that you're going from the strongest to the weakest note. If you can't figure out the order, don't worry as the result is the same.

Mode	Step 1	Step 2	Step 3	Step 4	Step 5	Chords
Ionian	1, 3, 5	7	6	2	4	M, M7
Dorian	1, b3, 5	6	b7	2	4	m, m7
Phrygian	1, b3, 5	b2	b7	b6	4	m, m7
Mixolydian	1, 3, 5	b7	6	2	4	7, 9
Aeolian	1, b3, 5	b6	b7	2	4	m, m7
Locrian	1, b3, b5	b2	b7	b6	4	dim, m7b5

Scale Formulas

Here are a few more formulas to try out from some of my favorite scales:

Melodic Minor: 1, 2, b3, 4, 5, 6, 7

Harmonic Minor: 1, 2, b3, 4, 5, b6, 7

Hungarian Minor: 1, 2, b3, #4, 5, b6, 7

Lydian Dominant: 1, 2, 3, #4, 5, 6, b7

Phrygian Dominant: 1, b2, 3, 4, 5, b6, b7

Mixolydian b6: 1, 2, 3, 4, 5, b6, b7

Harmonic Major: 1, 2, 3, 4, 5, b6, 7

More from Unlock the Guitar

Visit www.unlocktheguitar.net for more insight into all things guitar on the **blog**, and our extensive selection of eBooks on scales, chords, and the bestselling guitar hacks series.

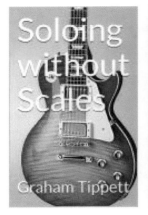  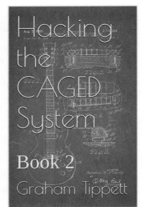 

  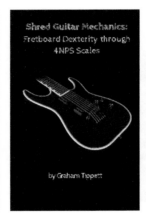 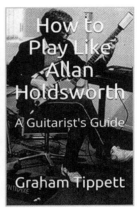

Made in the USA
Columbia, SC
03 September 2017